SU
& ANALYSIS
OF
WHO WE ARE
AND
HOW WE GOT HERE

Ancient DNA and the New Science
of the Human Past

A GUIDE TO THE BOOK
BY DAVID REICH

NOTE: This book is a summary and analysis and is meant as a companion to, not a replacement for, the original book.

Please follow this link to purchase a copy of the original book: https://amzn.to/2LmkwH4

Copyright © 2018 by ZIP Reads. All rights reserved. This book or parts thereof may not be reproduced in any form, stored in any retrieval system, or transmitted in any form by any means—electronic, mechanical, photocopy, recording, or otherwise—without prior written permission of the publisher, except as provided by United States of America copyright law. This book is intended as a companion to, not a replacement for the original book. ZIP Reads is wholly responsible for this content and is not associated with the original author in any way.

TABLE OF CONTENTS

SYNOPSIS 7

PART I: THE DEEP HISTORY OF OUR SPECIES 9

Chapter 1: The Genome, Ancestry, and DNA 9

Key Takeaway: All modern humans share common DNA from Africa. 10

Key Takeaway: We still know very little about the genome... 10

Key Takeaway: For every generation you look back, DNA is further diluted by the pool of ancestors. 11

Key Takeaway: Genome-wide association studies provide evidence for natural selection. 12

Chapter 2: Neanderthals & Humans 13

Key Takeaway: Ancient DNA analysis confirms Neanderthals interbred with modern humans. 13

Key Takeaway: Chromosomal changes allow for the dating of population mixtures. 14

Key Takeaway: Neanderthal DNA was further diluted due to lowered intermixed fertility rates. 14

Chapter 3: Ancient Humans Cohabitate 15

Key Takeaway: At some point, likely around 400,000 to 280,000 years, the Denisovans split into two distinct lineages. 16

Key Takeaway: Neanderthals, Denisovans, and modern humans did not all evolve directly from Homo erectus. 16

Key Takeaway: There were at least four distinct, divergent human populations living within the last 70,000 years. 17

Key Takeaway: Interbreeding with Denisovans and Neanderthals provided beneficial evolutionary traits to modern humans. 17

Key Takeaway: Evidence points to a "ghost" population of superarchaic humans. 18

Key Takeaway: Proposed timeline of human evolution: 18

Key Takeaway: Anatomically modern humans may not have evolved in Africa. 19

Key Takeaway: New discoveries continue to alter the foundations of what we think we know. 20

PART II: HOW WE GOT TO WHERE WE ARE TODAY 22

Chapter 4: Pre-European Ancestry 22

Key Takeaway: A ghost population of "Ancient North Eurasians" gave way to modern Native Americans and Europeans. 22

Key Takeaway: Modern "races" are not caused by genetic isolation over time, but by continued mixing. 23

Key Takeaway: A ghost population predated Mal'ta, European hunter-gatherers, and East Asians 23

Key Takeaway: Geneticists have reconstructed 35,000 years of human movement throughout Eurasia. 24

Key Takeaway: Modern concepts of race have no historical, genetic basis. 24

Chapter 5: Europe 25

Key Takeaway: Yamnaya culture—which saw the domestication of horses and the proliferation of the wheel— are the missing link to modern-day Europeans. 25

Key Takeaway: The Corded Ware culture was wrongly used as a justification for Nazi racial superiority. 26

Key Takeaway: Some cultures move both through the spread of people and the spread of ideas. 27

Key Takeaway: Indo-European languages were most likely spread by the Yamnaya. 27

Chapter 6: South Asia 28

Key Takeaway: India represents the meeting of east and west. 28

Key Takeaway: All of India's population is on a scale of western and eastern ancestry. 29

Key Takeaway: All of the mixing between ASI and ANI occurred within the last 4,000 years. 30

Key Takeaway: Endogamy and the caste system have created population bottlenecks of unique genetics all across India. ... 30

Key Takeaway: Both ANI and ASI Indians share a common ancestor. 31

Key Takeaway: Both Europeans and Indians were strongly influenced by the ancient steppe cultures. 31

Chapter 7: Native Americans 32

Key Takeaway: The "Clovis First" theory was proven wrong in 1997. 32

Key Takeaway: The vast majority of Native American populations share a common ancestor. 33

Key Takeaway: There are three distinct groups of Native Americans, but uncertainty clouds the field. 33

Key Takeaway: There is an additional genetic link between some Native Americans and Australasian populations. 34

Chapter 8: East Asians 34

Key Takeaway: The Southern Route hypothesis states that modern human ancestors migrated east across Asia before the Upper Paleolithic technology of 50,000 years ago. 34

Key Takeaway: Modern East Asians can be separated into three genetic clusters. 35

Key Takeaway: Austronesian language and Papuan ancestry define the Pacific island nations. 36

Key Takeaway: There is still much to learn about East Asian ancestry. 36

Chapter 9: Back to Africa 37

Key Takeaway: There was a mixture of archaic human and modern human in Africa around 300,000 years ago. 37

Key Takeaway: There were four great agricultural expansions in Africa. 37

Key Takeaway: An ancient ghost population in East Africa was displaced by the agriculturalists. 38

PART III: THE DISRUPTIVE GENOME 40

Chapter 10: Inequality in Genetics....................... 40

Key Takeaway: Genetic "Star Clusters" have a significant impact on future generations. 40

Key Takeaway: Genetic Sex Bias is evidenced in cultures throughout history around the world. 41

Chapter 11: Race and Identity in Genetics............. 42

Key Takeaway: There are genetic links to cognitive and behavioral traits—but caution must be exercised. 43

Key Takeaway: We must, as a society, find a new way to talk about genetic differences. 43

Key Takeaway: Results from genetic ancestry sites should be taken with a grain of salt. 44

Chapter 12: The Future of Ancient DNA 45

Key Takeaway: Radiocarbon dating was the biggest advancement in the history of archaeology—until ancient genome sequencing. 45

Key Takeaway: New methods must be used in order to fully understand more recent human history. 46

Key Takeaway: Ancient DNA could unlock secrets of human biology. 46

EDITORIAL REVIEW 48

BACKGROUND ON AUTHOR 50

SYNOPSIS

David Reich is a geneticist focused on the sequencing of ancient DNA in order to rebuild our conception of history, migration, and evolution. In his book, *Who We Are and How We Got Here* he credits Luca Cavalli-Sforza, the founder of the concept of genetic studies of the past, with all of his passion and success in the study of ancient genetics. Though most of Sforza's hypotheses have since been proven wrong, it was his vision that brought about the synthesis of linguistics, archaeology, history, and genetics.

The introduction presents an overview of the vast improvements in the ability to sequence the whole-genome DNA of ancient humans, growing the data set available from just five samples in 2010 to almost 4,000 in 2017, with many of the results as yet unpublished. In fact, the field is expanding so exponentially that by the time another study is published, the data set has often doubled once again. Reich credits this explosion of information with a breakthrough in the method of producing genome-wide DNA for ancient samples along with a precipitous drop in the cost per sample. He mostly credits his Harvard laboratory with the "ancient DNA revolution."

With his book, he argues that what they are uncovering is challenging long-held beliefs in linguistics, archaeology, history, and genetics alike. Most notably, he is quick to attack our preoccupation with genetic notions of race: the concept that a long time ago, each race was separated and genetically distinct before we migrated and began mixing. Though a theory previously ascribed to by many archaeologists, the advancements made have quickly disproven this notion. In fact, the genetic differences of ancient populations are just as mixed and mingled and diverse as current populations, if not more so.

The book is laid out in three sections, beginning with the earliest humans known on Earth, moving into more modern populations and how they came to be, and ends with an insightful commentary on the present and potential future of genetic sciences. While the science itself is both burgeoning and reliable, the politics surrounding the science remain fraught with overtones of racism, Nazism, and eugenics that humanity has been trying to escape since their shadowy reign in the early 20th century, and their troubling reemergence today.

Reich aims to provide the first glimpse into the vast knowledge being produced in this field that is accessible to the layman with detailed maps, graphs, and visualizations to help paint the picture of mass migrations of humans across the entire planet over hundreds of thousands of years. Never has more been known or understood about our ancient past—until now.

PART I: THE DEEP HISTORY OF OUR SPECIES

The very first page of the book is a timeline depicting the evolution of our species from our final break with chimpanzees approximately 5 to 7 million years ago.

3.2 million years ago, we see evidence of *Australopithecus* with the remains of "Lucy." 1.8 million years ago, fossils belonging to *Homo erectus* can be traced outside of Africa, in the countries of Georgia and Indonesia.

About 770,000–550,000 years ago is the estimate of when Neanderthals and modern humans genetically diverged.

320,000 years ago is the most recent ancestor of all modern-day humans. About 70,000–50,000 years ago we start seeing the divergence from Africa into West Africans, East Africans, West Eurasians, East Asians, and Native Americans.

CHAPTER 1: THE GENOME, ANCESTRY, AND DNA

The genome can be understood as a sequence of letters: ACGT (adenine, cytosine, guanine, thymine).

In one human cell, there are 46 chromosomes (23 each from maternal and paternal DNA). There are 2 genomes, one from each parent, and these genomes make up 3 billion pairs of nucleotides (The As, Cs, Gs, and Ts, consisting of 6 billion in total).

99.9% of DNA in humans is identical to one another; mutations are only found in .01% The mutations, or differences, found in that .01% tell us how closely two people are related to one another.

Mutations in DNA happen at a relatively stable rate, thus allowing the accumulation of mutations to act as a sort of clock, denoting roughly how much time has passed since two genomes were essentially the same.

Key Takeaway: All modern humans share common DNA from Africa.

Mitochondrial DNA—a type passed only through maternal lineage—sequenced from diverse people around the world in 1987 is what led scientists to the conclusion that the most recent maternal ancestor of all the genetic branches on the planet today split off around 200,000 years ago. This maternal link was given the name "Mitochondrial Eve."

Mitochondrial Eve negates "the multiregional hypothesis" believing that modern humans evolved separately, but concurrently, in Africa and Eurasia beginning about 1.8 million years ago. This means all humans today evolved from a much later expansion from Africa.

Key Takeaway: We still know very little about the genome.

50,000 years ago, Neanderthal humans experienced a vastly accelerated period of advancement in the use of complex language and tools, the likes of which had never been witnessed before. This period is known as the Late Stone or Upper Paleolithic Age. One of Reich's colleagues, Svante Pääbo dedicated himself to identifying any differences in the genome of modern and Neanderthal man that could explain this rapid growth. Essentially, Pääbo was looking to identify what makes humans human, in all of our inexplicable complexities. While he identified over a hundred thousand distinct differences, we are still ages away from understanding what they all mean.

Key Takeaway: For every generation you look back, DNA is further diluted by the pool of ancestors.

In 2001, the human genome was sequenced for the first time. By 2006, the process had advanced enough that sequencing was far cheaper. This allowed geneticists to look not just at the Y chromosome from the father and the mitochondrial DNA from the mother and try to piece things together, but to paint the entire picture—fully reconstructing thousands of lines of ancestral descent on each side.

Each of your cells contains the genomes of both of your parents; you are an amalgamation of those chromosomes, which are spliced uniquely with each generation to create the next. Your mother may have given you a quarter of her mother's DNA and three quarters of her father's. In total, your mother and father's genes will splice about 71 times per generation.

"One generation back, a person's genome is derived from about 118 (47 plus 71) stretches of DNA transmitted by his or her parents. Two generations back, the number of ancestral stretches of DNA grows to around 189 (47 plus 71 plus another 71) transmitted by four grandparents." (Reich, Kindle Locations 628-630).

The further back you go, the more certain it is that you have received no genetic material whatsoever from a portion of your ancestors. The idea of Mitochondrial Eve, a single mother of all the people, therefore, is quite a misnomer.

Key Takeaway: Genome-wide association studies provide evidence for natural selection.

Despite searching endlessly for a particular trigger of the Upper Paleolithic advancement, Reich believes that there isn't one specific gene or small group of mutations that led to this great leap forward. In fact, most of the studies he and his colleagues have performed point much more strongly towards natural selection. Genome-wide association studies look at genetic variances across entire populations, identifying where particular mutations split between groups—including variances in height, eye color, and even infant head size at birth. The question then becomes, if there wasn't a single mutation responsible for our rapid advancement 50,000 years ago, then was it natural selection? And how did it happen?

CHAPTER 2: NEANDERTHALS & HUMANS

Though we are alone as a subspecies on our planet today, there is evidence that modern humans once shared the planet with Neanderthals in Eurasia before they went extinct about 40,000 years ago. Despite common misconceptions, Neanderthals weren't monkeys who walked upright, but rather shared a capacity for abstract thinking and tool-making, though arguably not as advanced as their successor's.

Key Takeaway: Ancient DNA analysis confirms Neanderthals interbred with modern humans.

There has been much debate over whether Neanderthals interbred with modern humans, which, up until now could not be definitively answered using only the mitochondrial DNA that was available. In 2007, Reich and Pääbo discovered a rigorous, painstaking process that would allow them to sequence the entire Neanderthal genome from samples that were tens of thousands of years old. Their findings led to the conclusion that Neanderthals interbred the most with European, East Asian, and New Guinean populations, but also showed evidence of interbreeding among all non-African populations. That is to say, modern-day Africans are the only population that did *not* interbreed with Neanderthals, though some early Africans did.

Key Takeaway: Chromosomal changes allow for the dating of population mixtures.

If a Neanderthal man and a modern woman were to produce a child, that child would be given an unbroken Neanderthal chromosome and an unbroken human chromosome from each of their parents. In the process of splicing these chromosomes, the child would end up with 23 mixed chromosomes of varying degrees Neanderthal and human DNA. The Neanderthal DNA, however, remains in small chunks that are identifiable when mapping the chromosome. The more generations that pass, the smaller these "bits" of identifiable Neanderthal become, giving an indication of how many generations ago the two subspecies first interbred.

Key Takeaway: Neanderthal DNA was further diluted due to lowered intermixed fertility rates.

While Neanderthal DNA makes up 1-2% of most modern Europeans, Reich believed that that number should have been higher. He posited that the dilution of the DNA was based on the process of natural selection following the remixing of Neanderthal and human DNA after their initial evolutionary split. In fact, they found a "particularly intense depletion of Neanderthal ancestry by natural selection in two parts of the genome known to be relevant to the fertility of hybrids" (Reich, Kindle Locations 1133-1134).

Essentially, the X chromosome (one of the chromosomes for sex) carries a large number of markers for fertility. When the two distinct populations evolve independently, but then come back together, one of the results of their biological divergence is reduced fertility, often passed on through the X chromosome. Of course, natural selection would be inclined to remove any factors leading to reduced fertility. Since these chromosomes with lower fertility levels were coming more from the hybrid genome than the modern human genome, the hybrid chromosomes containing the Neanderthal DNA were disproportionately discarded in favor of the more fertile modern human.

CHAPTER 3: ANCIENT HUMANS COHABITATE

In 2008, a pinky bone was found in a cave in Russia.

The mitochondrial DNA from humans differs from Neanderthals by about 200 mutations. This pinky bone, however, carried more than 400 mutations from both modern humans *and* Neanderthals. Based on the rate of mutation, this bone was estimated to be more than 800,000 years old and to have belonged to a never-before-sampled group of archaic humans. This group, known as the Denisovans, split off from Neanderthal and modern humans even before they split about 470,000 to 360,000 years ago.

The only problem is that Denisovan DNA is closely related to modern New Guinean populations. More closely even than Neanderthals at 3–6% compared with only 2% Neanderthal. If the Denisovan pinky was found in Siberia, and New Guinean populations hail from islands in the South

Pacific...how did they meet without Denisovan DNA being as concentrated in mainland Asia?

Key Takeaway: At some point, likely around 400,000 to 280,000 years, the Denisovans split into two distinct lineages.

The data suggest that at some point the Siberian Denisovans split into what Reich refers to as the Australo-Denisovans, denoting their genetic concentration in Australia and New Guinea. This interbreeding potentially occurred in what is now Southeast Asia, China, or India, though they don't yet have the data to confirm this.

Key Takeaway: Neanderthals, Denisovans, and modern humans did not all evolve directly from *Homo erectus*.

It is tempting, Reich argues, to believe the "Out of Africa" theory in its entirety—that all modern humans came from the same genetic group that left Africa *en masse* millions of years ago. But the Denisovans prove that to be false. The oldest *Homo erectus* skeletons found out of Africa were 1.8 million years old in Dmanisi, Georgia and the island of Java in Indonesia around the same time. The genetic data tell us that the split of Denisovans from Neanderthals and modern humans was about 770,000 to 550,000 years ago. If the *Homo erectus* who left Africa was ancestral to those skeletons, the split would have to be at least as old.

Key Takeaway: There were at least four distinct, divergent human populations living within the last 70,000 years.

These populations are: modern humans, Neanderthals, Australo-Denisovans and Siberian Denisovans. Geneticists have mapped complete genomes of each of these subspecies, and it is likely that there are even more subspecies as yet to be identified. The evolutionary differences here are in the magnitude of hundreds of thousands of years, far more than any mutations apparent in the most-distantly separated lineages today: those from the San bushmen in Southern Africa, and basically everyone else.

Reich also briefly notes the Flores people who descended directly from *Homo erectus* in present-day Indonesia before the split into modern humans around 700,000 years ago. The Flores people, who were "hobbit-like" remained genetically distinct due to the deep waters separating them from the rest of humanity.

Key Takeaway: Interbreeding with Denisovans and Neanderthals provided beneficial evolutionary traits to modern humans.

Reich highlights the connection between Denisovan ancestry and modern Tibet: it is likely the Siberian-Denisovans contributed a mutation that provides a stronger adaptability to high altitudes, precipitating their occupation of the mountainous terrain beginning about 11,000 years ago.

Additionally, interbreeding with Neanderthals likely led to the strengthening of keratin proteins. Europeans and East-Asians have stronger markers of this Neanderthal DNA, presumably because skin and hair both require these proteins and would have been beneficial to survival.

Key Takeaway: Evidence points to a "ghost" population of superarchaic humans.

Because Sub-Saharan Africans are more closely related to Neanderthals than Denisovans, there is a missing link of interbreeding that is currently unexplained. Due to the amount of time it takes for a mutation to occur in 100% of a particular subspecies without the influence of natural selection—about a million years—the only way the Denisovans would not share this mutation is if their ancestors interbred with a divergent population. Reich posits that this superarchaic population represents a much deeper genetic separation than that between Denisovans, Neanderthals, and modern humans and occurred about 1.4 to 0.9 million years ago, after *Homo erectus* left Africa.

Key Takeaway: Proposed timeline of human evolution:

At least 1.8 million years ago: *Homo erectus* spread from Africa.

1.4 to 0.9 million years ago: *Homo erectus* lineage split away from modern human lineage, leading to the as-yet-unidentified "superarchaic humans." This subspecies also contributed significantly to the Denisovan DNA that shares a common ancestor with both Neanderthals and modern humans.

770,000 to 550,000 years ago: Modern humans separated from Neanderthals and Denisovans.

470,000 to 380,000 years ago: Neanderthals and Denisovans separated from each other.

Key Takeaway: Anatomically modern humans may not have evolved in Africa.

The theory that all modern humans originated in Africa is based on the knowledge that African DNA is currently the most divergent from all other present-day populations and that the oldest remains of an anatomically modern human (dated about 300,000 years ago) were found there.

Looking at what we know about ancient humans, however, many of the existing remains have been found in Eurasia. Perhaps Eurasia was a much hotter bed of evolutionary development than previously thought. Reich admits that this could be attributed to "ascertainment bias"—since most of the excavations are being done in Eurasia, that is where the remains are being found. But he also presents an alternative theory as to how this divergence played out.

In the traditional view, humans left Africa for Eurasia about 1.8 million years ago, followed by a second archaic lineage from Africa to Eurasia about 1.4 million years ago, followed by a third (the ancestors of Neanderthals and Denisovans) about 770,000 years ago, which led to present day Africans diverging from the modern humans who existed everywhere else.

In Reich's hypothesis, *Homo erectus* still leaves Africa for Eurasia 1.8 million years ago, but the ancestors of Denisovans, Neanderthals, and superarchaic humans develop outside of Africa, rather than within. Then, about 300,000 years ago, the ancestors of modern humans return to Africa. In Reich's model, only three major migrations are required, rather than four in the traditional model.

Modern humans aside, it is still widely agreed upon that Africa was the location of our original evolution from apes, and that *Homo erectus*, who directly preceded *Homo sapiens*, migrated from Africa about 1.8 million years ago.

Key Takeaway: New discoveries continue to alter the foundations of what we think we know.

In 2014, Pääbo and his colleagues sequenced mitochondrial DNA from the oldest human ever—over 400,000 years old—discovered in the Sima des los Huesos caves in Spain. Two years later, they published genome-wide data.

The Sima skeleton was of Neanderthal lineage, seemingly more closely related to Neanderthals than Denisovans. This proves that Neanderthal ancestors were already evolving in Europe at that time. Sima's mitochondrial DNA, however, appeared more closely related to Denisovan ancestry than Neanderthal. How could this be?

The most plausible theory Reich presents is that a group migrated out of Africa and mixed with the Sima population, replacing their mitochondrial DNA as more female partners were Denisovan and more male partners were in the Neanderthal lineage—creating the ancestors of true Neanderthals. This theory would also explain discrepancies in the timeline (about 200,000 years) dictated by the mitochondrial DNA and genome-wide analysis of the shared Neanderthal-modern-human ancestor.

Whatever the explanation, it would appear that Eurasia was a hotbed of evolutionary activity, that multiple subspecies of very similar human ancestors were migrating and interbreeding, and that we still have a lot to uncover.

PART II: HOW WE GOT TO WHERE WE ARE TODAY

CHAPTER 4: PRE-EUROPEAN ANCESTRY

For a long time, there has been a commonly held notion that the evolution of populations occurs like the branches of a tree: once a population splits off, it will be genetically distinct, and never "fuse" with the branch it split off from. This has been proven to be incorrect.

Key Takeaway: A ghost population of "Ancient North Eurasians" gave way to modern Native Americans and Europeans.

Northern Europeans share more ancestry with Native Americans than any other population today. Reich deduces the existence of a now-diluted "ghost race" that spread both east across the Bering land bridge to become Native Americans, and west to become modern Europeans. This race would have been as physically distinct as East Asians, West Eurasians, and Native Americans are today. Ancient North Eurasians were so successful that half of the world today gets between 5 and 40% of their genomes from their lineage. In 2013, they found human remains in Mal'ta, Siberia that were 24,000 years old; the remains confirmed their theory.

Key Takeaway: Modern "races" are not caused by genetic isolation over time, but by continued mixing.

The prevailing theory of the different races in the past century is that we all migrated out of Africa, landed where we are, and became genetically distinct tens of thousands of years ago, if not longer. This theory treats us all as branches on a tree with a single trunk. What the genome revolution has uncovered instead is that modern race is much more an amalgamation of races who lived previously, consistently mixing and migrating, diverging and rejoining. Not one race today is genetically isolated from the races of the past. It is less a tree with branches and more of a trellis—where every split can come back and cross the other again.

Key Takeaway: A ghost population predated Mal'ta, European hunter-gatherers, and East Asians

The ghost population, named "Basal Eurasians" split from the Eurasian lineage before that lineage split into Mal'ta, European hunter-gatherers, and East Asians. This lineage is still strongly represented, contributing about a quarter of the DNA of present-day Europeans and Near Easterners. Interestingly, the Basal Eurasians would appear to have little to no Neanderthal ancestry, suggesting that Basal Eurasians split off before Neanderthals began remixing with the majority of other non-Africans.

Key Takeaway: Geneticists have reconstructed 35,000 years of human movement throughout Eurasia.

1. Humans come out of Africa and the Near East 50,000 years ago. Ancient North Eurasians, East Asian, and Australian ancestors head east toward Asia.

2. European hunter-gatherers—a lineage that was uninterrupted for 20,000 years—spread to both Western Europe and Russia about 35,000 years ago.

3. In the Gravettian expansion, groups of European hunter-gatherers spread west towards present-day Italy and France until they were pushed out by expanding glaciers between 33,000 and 22,000 years ago.

4. A genetically distinct group from far-western Europe moved eastward about 19,000 years ago in the Magdalenian expansion.

5. Later migration, about 14,000 years ago during a period of warming after the last ice age homogenized the populations of Europe and the Near East.

Key Takeaway: Modern concepts of race have no historical, genetic basis.

Though today, much of West Eurasia (modern-day Europe, Central Asia, and the Middle East) is a relative genetic monoculture, this wasn't the case as recently as 10,000 years ago. West Eurasia at the time was divided into four distinct groups: the western part of the Near East (the Fertile Crescent), the eastern part (Iran), the hunter-gatherers of central and western Europe, and the hunter-gatherers of eastern Europe. These groups were as genetically different as Europeans and East Asians are today and would have been considered "races" by modern standards.

Our conception of race today as being a "pure" lineage is completely wrong. We are all descendants of mixed races that no longer exist, and we will likely continue to make new races in the future.

CHAPTER 5: EUROPE

"The extraordinary fact that emerges from ancient DNA is that just 5,000 years ago, the people who are now the primary ancestors of all extant northern Europeans had not yet arrived" (Reich, Kindle Location 2054).

Key Takeaway: Yamnaya culture—which saw the domestication of horses and the proliferation of the wheel—are the missing link to modern-day Europeans.

Prior to the Yamnaya culture about 5,000 years ago, Eurasia was comprised of four genetically separate groups of farmers and hunter-gatherers who surprisingly, did not interbreed as much as one would expect. These delineations remained in place in Eurasia from about 10,000 years ago, until the

Yamnaya came from the steppes of central Asia with their wheels and their horses. Modern-day Europeans, who could have been expected to be direct descendants of the farmers and hunter-gatherers before them, were missing a key piece of their ancestry. This piece was provided by the Yamnaya. The Yamnaya themselves were a mix of DNA from what is now Armenia and Iran, before migrating north from the Caucasus.

Key Takeaway: The Corded Ware culture was wrongly used as a justification for Nazi racial superiority.

Before the genome revolution, archeologists were primarily responsible for deducing the movement of people and cultures. One such way is through the items they left behind. The Corded Ware culture—named for the twine they wove into their pottery—left their mark across most of Europe and were believed to be of German descent. Before the second World War, this was used as evidence that the German people were superior and had ancient claim to lands to the east.

What we now know is that the Corded Ware culture were actually a westward expansion of the Yamnaya who genetically displaced the western Europeans farmers occupying present-day Germany, not a superior pre-German race who conquered everything from Russia westward. Any concepts of the Yamnaya representing a "pure" Aryan culture are further muddied by the fact that the Yamnaya mixed with the Corded Ware who further mixed with the Bell Beaker culture, who then spread across the continent.

Key Takeaway: Some cultures move both through the spread of people and the spread of ideas.

The Bell Beaker culture, known for their bell-shaped drinking glasses, left evidence of their prevalence across Europe into Iberia and Great Britain. But unlike the Corded Ware culture, places with archaeological evidence of the Bell Beaker culture do not always share ancestry, indicating that different peoples adopted their ideas without mixing genetically. The Bell Beaker culture spread across Europe mostly in this manner until it moved into Britain, which is the first known occurrence of steppe ancestry on the British Isles, about 4,500 years ago.

It is important to note that steppe ancestry didn't just mix into existing British lineage, it practically replaced it. Skeletons from the Bronze Age (after the Beaker culture) have 90% steppe ancestry, where the people who built Stonehenge had none.

Key Takeaway: Indo-European languages were most likely spread by the Yamnaya.

Previous hypotheses by linguists and archaeologists attributed the spread of Indo-European languages—which are too similar to not have come from a shared root language—to the migration of Anatolian (present-day Turkey) farmers about 9,000 years ago. The data disagree. The language was most likely to have come from the Yamnaya 5,000 years ago who spread not only westward into Europe, but also southward into present-day India.

CHAPTER 6: SOUTH ASIA

The *Rig Veda* is an ancient Sanskrit text, and the oldest text in Hinduism, that may hold secrets of population movement across India and South Asia, as well as the collapse of the Indus Valley Civilization. It may also provide evidence that some South Asian cultures and religions were influenced by Indo-European Eurasia including Iran, Greece, and Scandinavia.

Key Takeaway: India represents the meeting of east and west.

Most of northern India speaks Indo-European languages, related to the languages of Iran and Europe. Southern India speaks Dravidian languages, not closely related to languages outside of South Asia. Some of northeastern India speaks Sino-Tibetan languages. India was likely the first place where western farming practices met with Chinese rice and millet farming.

Key Takeaway: All of India's population is on a scale of western and eastern ancestry.

Disproving a theory that Indians and Chinese evolved from a singular group of ancestors, or that Indians and Europeans came from a single group, the data suggest that India is a genetic scale with both European and Han Chinese influence. The western influencing ancestry is referred to as West Eurasians and includes populations from Europe, the Near East, and central Asia. The second is influenced by East Asians. While everyone they tested on mainland India had some level of West Eurasian ancestry (from as low as 20 to as high as 80%), the population of Little Andaman island—which has been geographically isolated for tens of thousands of years—had none. The population of little Andaman allowed them to see how far the mainland population had mixed with other "races" in the past.

Due to political considerations, Reich's findings that most Indians were related to Europeans were not easily accepted. As such, they renamed the ancestors of the two distinct groups as "Ancestral North Indians" (ANI, who share the DNA of Europeans, central Asians, and Near Easterners) and "Ancestral South Indians" (ASI, who share relation to a population that no longer exists today).

The conclusion: everyone in India today is a mix, and no group can claim genetic purity.

Key Takeaway: All of the mixing between ASI and ANI occurred within the last 4,000 years.

Just as the Indus Valley Civilization was collapsing, and the *Rig Veda* was composed, there was a profound mixing of previously segregated populations.

As they looked at this mixing, ANI ancestry was found to be associated with higher social status in the caste system. ANI ancestry also derives more from the male Y-chromosome than the female mitochondrial DNA. This tells us that males with a higher social status had more access to females from lower castes, a pattern we see repeat itself throughout history.

Key Takeaway: Endogamy and the caste system have created population bottlenecks of unique genetics all across India.

The data show that endogamy (marrying only within your group) in many of the *jati*, or Indian subgroups, has been upheld for thousands of years. Despite living in highly-mixed populations based on location, there has been little to no intermixing with Indians from another *jati*. If there had been only a 1% mixture, these bottlenecks would not exist today. Though India seems like a large population, the reality is that the subcontinent is made up a large number of small, genetically distinct populations.

Key Takeaway: Both ANI and ASI Indians share a common ancestor.

Of the three groups believed to have contributed to modern-day Indians—ancient steppe cultures, Little Andaman Islanders, and ancient Iranian farmers—the Iranian farmers contributed significantly to both genetically distinct ANI and ASI Indians.

The ANI were a mix of about 50% steppe ancestry (distantly related to the Yamnaya) and 50% Iranian-farmer.

The ASI had no influence from the Yamnaya but were about 25% earlier Iranian farmers and about 75% from established hunter-gatherers of South Asia who no longer exist.

Key Takeaway: Both Europeans and Indians were strongly influenced by the ancient steppe cultures.

What the data have shown us is that the Yamnaya and other ancient cultures of the central Asian steppes had a significant impact on both the Indian and European subcontinents. These cultures brought with them farming practices as well as the spread of Indo-European language and religion between 9,000 and 4,000 years ago. How exactly the Indus Valley Civilization came to be about 4,500 to 3,800 years ago, and what their genetic mix was, remains a mystery geneticists are eager to solve.

CHAPTER 7: NATIVE AMERICANS

The presiding theory over the habitation of the Americas was that a singular group entered sometime around 13,000 years ago, when the "ice-free corridor" was created, allowing ancient humans to access the continent for the first time across the land bridge formed over what is now the Bering Strait. Evidence of a culture known as Clovis, who used tools and hunted mammoths, mastodons, and bison, has been found over hundreds of sites in North America.

Key Takeaway: The "Clovis First" theory was proven wrong in 1997.

With the discovery of a site in Monte Verde, Chile, the presiding theory was disproven. Definitive evidence surfaced for a "pre-Clovis" people existing in the Americas at least 14,000 years ago, preceding the ice-free zone. These people had differently-styled tools and likely reached South America via the coastline, leaving behind sites that were then swallowed by rising sea levels.

Genetic data shows us two distinct groups: The Clovis, who gave rise to most of the native populations in South and Mesoamerica, and the second, who today live in eastern and central Canada.

Key Takeaway: The vast majority of Native American populations share a common ancestor.

These "First Americans" migrated (in theory) into a human-less land, spreading wildly before later diverging into the genetically distinct groups we see today. Unlike the Eurasian peoples, these groups seem to have branched off from one genetic tree trunk as they moved south, settled, and, for the most part, never re-mixed with subsequent populations. This can be seen in the genetic distinction of people from Peru, Argentina, and even islands off British Columbia.

Key Takeaway: There are three distinct groups of Native Americans, but uncertainty clouds the field.

Based on the spread of language and new genetic analysis, Native Americans can be split into the First Americans, Na-Dene speakers, and Eskimo-Aleut speakers. The First Americans attributed about 90% of the DNA in Na-Dene speakers and 60% in Eskimo-Aleut, confirming that most Native Americans share a common ancestor. Unfortunately, due to political issues surrounding the study of Native Americans in the contiguous United States, data are limited, and tribes are extremely cautious of letting their DNA be studied. As such, there are many gaps in understanding still to be filled.

Key Takeaway: There is an additional genetic link between some Native Americans and Australasian populations.

This ghost population, called Population Y, have descendants found mostly in Amazonia, and appear to have no genetic link to the Clovis infant remains of 13,000 years ago. This population may disprove the theory that the First Americans arrived on an unpopulated continent and suggests instead that they mixed with Population Y, mostly replaced them, and that only in Amazonia did this genetic marker remain strong due to geographical barriers.

CHAPTER 8: EAST ASIANS

East Asia is home to some of the earliest humans known in the world—at least 1.7 million years old found in China and Indonesia. East Asia was home to a population of archaic humans. Modern humans appeared to have arrived in Australia, Europe, and East Asia at around the same time.

Key Takeaway: The Southern Route hypothesis states that modern human ancestors migrated east across Asia before the Upper Paleolithic technology of 50,000 years ago.

This hypothesis is now widely accepted. The question isn't whether or not there were modern humans outside of Africa over 50,000 years ago, but what effect they had on current populations. The Southern Route refers to the path they supposedly took along the southern coast of Asia. The genetics here show that Chinese and Australians share almost all of their ancestry with a homogenous population who separated earlier from the ancestors of Europeans.

Key Takeaway: Modern East Asians can be separated into three genetic clusters.

These clusters are: those living in the Amur River basin on the border between China and Russia, those on the Tibetan Plateau, and those in Southeast Asia.

The Southeast Asian populations are likely to have come from a "Yangtze River Ghost Population" who separated and spread rice farming techniques across the region. This ghost population mixed with existing hunter-gatherer populations that still contribute genetically to Southeast Asians today.

The Han Chinese, however do not share the same ancestry. They instead have a shared ancestry (and Sino-Tibetan languages) that spread to the Tibetan Plateau about 3,600 years ago. This ancestry is independent from the influences in Southeast Asia and has been named the "Yellow River Ghost Population." These two ghost populations split off and spread about 10,000 to 5,000 years ago.

Key Takeaway: Austronesian language and Papuan ancestry define the Pacific island nations.

Evidence shows that East Asian farming spread first to Taiwan around 4,000 years ago, and then expanded to much of the Pacific islands including the Philippines, Vanuatu, and as far east as Tonga and Samoa before finally making its way to New Zealand, Hawaii, and Easter Island as recently as 800 years ago. This expansion also reaches as far west as Madagascar. All of these Austronesian populations have a close genetic link to the aboriginal Taiwanese. The Papuan ancestry that is found in such a high percent of Pacific islanders, however, was proven to have come from two successive migrations, as opposed to the one mass expansion of Papuan DNA as previously thought.

Key Takeaway: There is still much to learn about East Asian ancestry.

Due to strict laws surrounding the removal of biological material from Asian countries, much of the ancient DNA revolution has yet to reach their shores. Reich, however, is optimistic; the science is spreading rapidly in China, and he is hopeful that we will soon have as clear a picture of Han Chinese and Austronesian ancestry as we do of European lineages.

CHAPTER 9: BACK TO AFRICA

Since modern humans left Africa and evolved mostly independently from Africans, it is tempting for scientists to disregard Africa as if it has remained genetically unchanged in the last 50,000 years. Of course, this isn't true, and Africa has its own unique evolution and interbreeding from archaic humans to modern man.

Key Takeaway: There was a mixture of archaic human and modern human in Africa around 300,000 years ago.

Based on rare genetic mutations across populations, geneticists have discovered that all non-Africans, and even divergent African lineages, descended from this mixture. This mixture is so even—approximately 50/50 in the samples they have—it suggests an unclear distinction between which is modern and which is archaic.

Key Takeaway: There were four great agricultural expansions in Africa.

About 4,000 years ago, a farming culture was formed in west-central Africa. About 2,500 years ago, it spread to Lake Victoria in eastern Africa and involved iron toolmaking. By 1,700 years ago, it had reached southern Africa. This migration was also responsible for the spread of Bantu languages and is known as the Bantu expansion.

The Nilo-Saharan expansion followed the expansion of the Sahara Desert in the last 5,000 years and was driven not only by farmers, but by cattle herders such as the Maasai of Kenya and Tanzania as well.

Another agricultural expansion (bringing both farming technology and language) spread from the Near East back into Africa around 7,000 years ago. The movement of Afroasiatic language and the limited genetic data available suggest that Ethiopia and Somalia share a common ancestor with Near East farmers from 10,000 years ago. Meaning that the migration was back in to Africa, rather than simply out to Eurasia.

The fourth expansion is based on the click languages of southern Africa, known as Khoe-Kwadi. These languages were believed to have originated in East Africa before migrating south along with herding practices as has been seen in 1,200-year-old remains of a South African who presented a mix of San hunter-gatherer and Khoe-Kwadi DNA.

Key Takeaway: An ancient ghost population in East Africa was displaced by the agriculturalists.

This population, named the East African Foragers, contribute significantly to the DNA of Ethiopians, Kenyans, and present-day Hadza of Tanzania. They are also more closely related to non-Africans than other sub-Saharan Africans. This suggests they may have been the people in the

Middle to Later Stone Age transition, propelling them out to Eurasia.

The East African Foragers were actually split into three separate genetic groups with varying ancestry pre-dating the Bantu expansion across the African continent. This ancestry is shared in degrees in peoples from South Africa to Zanzibar and Ethiopia and is another testament to the constant mixing, moving, and remixing present in Africa for tens and hundreds of thousands of years.

PART III: THE DISRUPTIVE GENOME

Reich devotes the final section of the book to more modern genetic queries, including the history of West Africans in the Americas following slavery, what modern-day Americans may look like from a genetic standpoint, and the role of the genome revolution in race relations, culture, and society.

CHAPTER 10: INEQUALITY IN GENETICS

Key Takeaway: Genetic "Star Clusters" have a significant impact on future generations.

A star cluster is a group of individuals over time who appear to share a common paternal ancestor. This is evidenced in the Y-chromosome type believed to be from a single male—likely quite powerful—who fathered many more children than most, leaving an indelible mark on the genetics of history. Genghis Khan, as well as an Irish warlord from medieval Ireland, have both left star clusters that have been recorded.

Also important for star clusters were the Yamnaya, who were believed to have had a highly stratified and male-centric society. The genetic makeup of generations who followed the Yamnaya show much more diversity in maternal, mitochondrial DNA than in the paternal lines.

Key Takeaway: Genetic Sex Bias is evidenced in cultures throughout history around the world.

One conclusion that Reich has reached again and again is that the Y chromosome will be stronger in groups with higher social standing. That is, males, in every socially stratified group he has studied, have a stronger prevalence with women of lower social status—whether it be with the higher-ranked ANI Indians or white males and African-born slave women in the 19th century. Analysis has shown that European ancestry in a modern day African American is about four times as likely to have come from a male ancestor than a female one. This divide was likely much higher before the cultural acceptance of mixed-race relationships since the Civil Rights Movement.

This pattern presents itself everywhere from the Yamnaya to the Bantu and Pygmies of west-central Africa to the Europeans invading South and Central Americans.

One notable exception to the Y-chromosome bias is in Pacific island cultures. While most of their Papuan ancestry came from later waves of migration from west to east mixing with mainland East Asian ancestry, the Papuan side of their genetics more strongly favors mitochondrial DNA. That is to say, the native females produced more offspring than the newly-arrived males.

CHAPTER 11: RACE AND IDENTITY IN GENETICS

Genetic research into biological differences between races can be very useful for identifying genes that cause higher prevalence of disease. Unfortunately, some research that Reich presented locating specific genes that caused higher rates of prostate cancer in Americans with African descent versus European-American descent was dismissed as racist. Regardless, race as we know it is still a useful tool for doctors when diagnosing patients. Africans and their descendants are far more likely to have sickle cell anemia among other ailments. Similar penchants, such as the prevalence of Tay-Sachs disease in Ashkenazi Jews, are well-documented in genetic science.

While biological genetics is a convenient haven for white supremacists, scientists don't have the luxury of pretending there aren't any differences from one race to the next, even if some will attempt to use that science in the same way Hitler did.

Ultimately, Reich argues that we have to move past the false dichotomy that any discussion of biological race is Nazism, and the other side that any differences between races are so genetically small that they must all be ignored. Like most things in life, the reality is somewhere in the middle.

Key Takeaway: There are genetic links to cognitive and behavioral traits—but caution must be exercised.

Though dangerous to discuss, Reich presents findings that genetics can predict physical characteristics like skin color and height as well as behavioral and emotional ones such as educational attainment and IQ scores. While he understands this kind of research could be abused and misrepresented in the wrong hands, it is no more beneficial for science to ignore it. He argues that our current races, while genetically different enough to warrant classification, came from races that no longer exist. The fact that Europeans and Native Americans share a common ancestor is argument enough that current notions of race and superiority aren't legitimate. No one race can claim an objective superiority over another as we all evolved from the same, now extinct, races.

These genetic predictors of educational attainment, however, have been wrongly used to justify everything from eugenics in the 1950s to modern-day defenses of genetically inferior peoples that, unsurprisingly, align with existing racial stereotypes. Much of the "science" presented in these "master race" arguments is patently false.

Key Takeaway: We must, as a society, find a new way to talk about genetic differences.

Burying our heads in the sand isn't going to make genetic research disappear. It's likely that the genome revolution will continue to provide a plethora of genetically-based evidence for different traits across different cultures. What we must do is find an inclusive way to discuss these findings rather than pretend they don't exist or allow Neo-Nazis to drive the rhetoric surrounding modern genetics.

One of the key things to remember is that **genetic differences are greater within populations than between them.** Any one person in a society can excel at a trait that their particular people aren't genetically endowed with on average; genetically predicted performance won't always match actual performance. Instead of making judgments on someone's ability because we know their ethnic group has a propensity for a particular skill, why don't we treat every person as an individual and see what they themselves are capable of?

Key Takeaway: Results from genetic ancestry sites should be taken with a grain of salt.

Despite the wild increase in popularity of sites like 23andMe and Ancestry.com, the results aren't always as accurate as you may think. For African Americans especially, there has been so much intermixing in the population since their ancestors were brought over that there can be little definitive understanding of their true African roots. Yet these companies are more than happy to tell you with certainty your people hail from one ancient tribe or another. This problem extends itself to non-African populations as well, where 23andMe is providing grossly inaccurate

"Neanderthal mutation percentages," despite the variations in most people being less than a few tenths of a percent.

CHAPTER 12: THE FUTURE OF ANCIENT DNA

Key Takeaway: Radiocarbon dating was the biggest advancement in the history of archaeology—until ancient genome sequencing.

With the discovery of radiocarbon dating in 1950, archaeology was transformed from a branch of the humanities to a legitimate, science-based field. Until that point, estimates of the ages of artifacts were at best a guessing game. With this advancement, archaeologists could prove beyond doubt when an artifact was from, offering new insights into old discoveries and shattering previously held beliefs about the ages of ancient cultures.

With the dawn of genome sequencing, archaeological assumptions on the movement of people based on artifacts can be definitively challenged. Once again, long-held theories are being proven wrong, and science is forced to accept the new truths that come with every new technology. Reich compares the importance of genetic sequencing to human knowledge to the completion of mostly accurate world maps in the 15th and 16th centuries—they changed they way we see the world.

Key Takeaway: New methods must be used in order to fully understand more recent human history.

The methods that Reich and his team use to study ancient populations work because so much time has passed since they existed, and the following populations are sufficiently differentiated. In just the last 4,000 years, many more waves of migration have occurred that are yet to be fully mapped from a genetic perspective. Reich believes mapping these more recent shifts in human populations will give us more insight not only into our own development since the dawn of writing and empires, but also a better understanding of the relative sizes of populations throughout history.

Key Takeaway: Ancient DNA could unlock secrets of human biology.

One of the more difficult applications of ancient DNA is to help us understand our biological evolution—the mutating of our genes as a response over time to different stimuli. Sample sizes of ancient DNA are currently too small to perform such an analysis (thousands in each unique subgroup would be needed, we currently only have a handful from each), but Reich is optimistic about reaching these numbers in the future with advancements in ancient sequencing technology.

Understanding the development of these mutations could tell us whether humans evolved more quickly or more slowly since the agricultural revolution. It could answer the question of if modern science has slowed natural selection in an age where the infertile can have children, the disabled can be mobile, and the near-blind can see—genetic mutations that would have meant the end of the line for early humans. Only time, and science, will tell.

EDITORIAL REVIEW

David Reich's book, *Who We Are and How We Got Here: Ancient DNA and the New Science of the Human Past* is a detailed presentation of everything geneticists know about ancient DNA to date. At his own admission, the findings in this book could likely be outdated before the time of publication—that's how quickly the field is developing.

While Reich's book is meant as a layman's guide, it doesn't lack the technical side needed to understand what he is presenting. His explanations of genetic science, sequencing, and techniques are dense, though comprehensible with a little effort. Though this summary provides only the findings of his research, he thoroughly details his methods, processes, and deductions. He credits many of his colleagues throughout the book for various findings and is the first to admit when there is a missing link, or something they still just don't know. In these cases, he provides all current working theories to the reader.

The findings he presents are often difficult to pull from the convoluted and confusing histories, following populations you have never heard of moving back and forth across continents over hundreds of thousands and even millions of years, splitting and rejoining again and again. To aid in understanding, there are plenty of timelines and graphics to paint a clearer picture of the of the history he and other geneticists have discovered.

Beyond all the science, Reich devotes a significant portion of the book to discussing ancient genetics from an ethical perspective and is careful to stand his ground while not crossing any lines. While there are plenty who say today "there is no biological basis for race" Reich argues that this isn't exactly true, though what they have learned certainly disproves any previously-held notions of racial purity. Reich argues fervently that we embrace the development of both modern and ancient genetics openly in order to better diagnose disease, and to better understand our own biological development. Despite the issue being fraught with these racial and political motives, he insists there is a productive way to discuss these delicate topics, which are mired in bloody history, without succumbing to notions of genetic superiority.

Whatever your ethical point of view, the revelations the book presents are truly captivating. They will, undoubtedly, change your perceptions of people, race, and ancient cultures. At the very least, they will have you curious about the results of your own 23andMe analysis. Reich's book may be the first of its kind in the field, but there is no doubt many more will be published in the decades to come.

BACKGROUND ON AUTHOR

David Emil Reich is a geneticist known for his work on ancient populations. He received his B.A. in physics from Harvard and his PhD in zoology from Oxford. He is currently an associate at the Broad Institute, whose research studies compare the human genome to chimpanzees, Neanderthals, and Denisovans. He is a professor of genetics at Harvard Medical School and a Howard Hughes Medical Institute Investigator. He has contributed significant research to the field of genetics including on the split of chimpanzees and early humans, his work on the ANI and ASI populations in India, and the interbreeding of humans and Neanderthals, among others. His work has been published in numerous scientific journals.

Who We Are and How We Got Here: Ancient DNA and the New Science of the Human Past is his first book.

END OF BOOK SUMMARY

*If you enjoyed this **ZIP Reads** publication, we encourage you to purchase a copy of the original book from.*

We'd also love an honest review on Amazon.com!

Made in the USA
Middletown, DE
09 January 2019